KV-118-202

BLER

Please renew or return items by the date shown on your receipt

www.hertsdirect.org/libraries

Renewals and enquiries: 0300 123 4049

Textphone for hearing or speech impaired   0300 123 4041

Hertfordshire

468 833 85 9

Your Sax Is On Fire

I was born to a family of Canadian Geese in 1975. They soon disowned me before I became the circuit to the European Grand Prix in the late 1970s. Blah blah blah blah. Does anybody ever read this section?

"Your Sax Is On Fire" is a collection of quirky, irreverent, and surreal poems about the world we live in today.

I hope you enjoy the collection, but if you don't then please use the book as a coaster, or a milkfloat.

Matador
9 Priory Business Park
Wistow Road
Kibworth Beauchamp
Leicester LE8 0RX, UK
Tel: (+44) 116 279 2299
Fax: (+44) 116 279 2277
Email: books@troubador.co.uk
Web: www.troubador.co.uk/matador

http://georgestanworth.webeden.co.uk/

ISBN 978 1780880 273

British Library Cataloguing in Publication Data.
A catalogue record for this book is available from the British Library.

Typeset in 11pt Aldine 401 BT Roman by Troubador Publishing Ltd, Leicester, UK

Matador is an imprint of Troubador Publishing Ltd

Printed in Great Britain by the MPG Books Group, Bodmin and King's Lynn

Contents

Speed-Dating

We met.

You wept.

I left.

I'm Not Gordon Ramsay You Know!

A Custard Cream

was not your dream

meal for a first date.

You called me mean

but if I'd been

I'd have cooked

an 'After Eight!'

An IT Contractor Works Harder Than Most

Making a coffee, moving a file,

taking a phone call once in a while.

Going on Facebook, chatting to friends,

checking the latest mortgage rate trends.

    An IT Contractor works harder than most.

Looking at YouTube, gasping out 'Wow'.

Telling a colleague you're busy right now.

Drawing a picture. Staying awake.

Thinking about your next summer break.

    An IT Contractor works harder than most.

Cleaning out email, having a tweet.

Downloading music, having a sweet.

Solving a problem by logging a call,

with outside suppliers, you give it your all.

    An IT Contractor works harder than most.

Making a coffee, having a chat,

building a network – you're brilliant at that!

Moaning how others do not pull their weight,

and how you deserve a longer lunch break.

    An IT Contractor bullsh★★s more than most.

Replacement UPVC Advent Calendar Windows

They all fell out

on Joseph.

The 3 wise men

were good-

but not at

double glazing!

Their gifts

were putty,

frames and glass,

how the stable boy did laugh.

The tabloids

claimed the star

was drinking like a footballer.

It dimmed for 40 chocolate years –

then died from hypothermia.

Your Sax Is On Fire

I scream and I shout

'Put it out, put it out.

Her sax is on fire.'

You brand me a liar

and call it a crime,

you get half a dozen such calls all the time.

'Please tell her Deliah,

your sax is on fire!'

I hand you the phone, but the line has gone dead.

(I wish your viola was burning instead.)

Florence and the Washing Machine

The worst cover band ever.
  They did not gel together.
    They didn't drum or try to sing.
      They only put their washing in
        the machine.
          How obscene!

  It cost me twenty pound
    to hear their sound
      and see their smalls
        spin round and round
          and round.

  It was as dull as ovaltine
    or Sage Against the Fruit Machine.

Marina and the Seven of Diamonds

Marina, you try very hard

but once again that's not my card.

Your magic we don't really dig.

We came here for a music gig.

The nine of spades you quickly say.

I lie and shout out 'Yes, hooray!'.

You take a bow to mute applause

as elephants block all the doors.

A customer asks where's my train?

I'm in a different world again!

Bacardi Geezer

The landlord of the 'Sleepy Bore'
hadn't run a pub before.
He didn't have much common sense.
(He put the tampons in the gents,)

then placed urinals in the ladies,
(no wonder they kept having babies.)
The cash point blocked the fire door
and pool was played upon the floor.

The drinks were served in Tupperware
by staff straight out of Mothercare.
Ready Salted was the main meal.
The bouncers looked like Ian Beale.

The happy hour was all wrong.
It only lasted for one song.
Mainly as the singers fled,
when darts were played above their head.

The jukebox only took 1p's

and jumped on songs with Bs and Es.

'Bye Bye Baby' sounded street –

Y Y Ay is Geordie speak!

The games machine had gonnorhea.

The fruit was off, so too the beer.

The landlord of the 'Sleepy Bore'

isn't at his pub no more.

He had amnesia and forgot where he lived.

I SAY I SAY I SWAY

You told a joke,

and then one more

before you fell down on the floor.

We said that you should sober up.

You said, 'Shut up'.

We picked you up.

Smelling of rum

and stale chewing gum,

(plus Pedigree Chum);

you stuck two fingers in the air

and reached for Scotch in underwear.

Once again this was your greeting....

As you chaired the rather contrived 'Don't drink at work,
Nuclear Safety, Best Practices for Brain Surgeons, and
How to look after your liver' annual meeting.

PUBSTRIFE

He only sells sherry and gin.

(No wonder his custom is thin.)

He's never run bars in the past.

(He better start learning damn fast.)

He plays DVDs of the news

and places dart boards in the loos.

His raffle prize is a mince pie,

at Christmas and even July.

The landlord says things aren't too great.

I tell him I'm not surprised really if you're interrupting
poems written by your customers. Cheers mate!

AN ASBO FOR SOME WAS NEVER ENOUGH

Clarkson loud music chundered around.

Alsatians' barking injured the sound.

Empties of Bailey's smashed on the ground.

An ASBO for some was never enough!

Random expletives yelled for effect;

stealing from family to pay off their debt.

Jeremy Kyle was soon to be met.

An ASBO for some was never enough!

You went off to Spain to help you calm down,

and extra tax credits were given by Brown.

You used them wisely defacing the town.

Two ASBO's for some was never enough!

If The Government Created The World

'The moon and stars are running late,

of course we don't feel shame.

The last administration

are the only one's to blame.

The birds and bees consignment

has not arrived on time.

We've got a billion flies instead,

but no one will resign.

The sky's not yet constructed,

it's got a major crack.

We'll have to put a tax on air

to get our money back.

Stars and space are running late,
of course we don't feel shame.
The last administration
are the only one's to blame.

The project's over budget,
we've cut back on some trees.
If you would like more nature
you'll have to pay the fees.

We'll take away your water
if you say we're unkind.
I know we said we wouldn't,
but now we've changed our minds.

We've all been made imperfect,
just like each Lord and Dame.
The last administration
are the only one's to blame.'

THE MASSIVE PASSIVE

I'm sorry to inform you

that things will not improve,

because the good are passive

and the rest would not approve.

You're fed up waiting for your train.

It's always running late.

But think it's inappropriate

lodging a complaint.

They're taking full advantage.

They know we hate to fuss.

They take great satisfaction

from the passiveness of us.

Changes will not happen

unless we make a stand.

No more massive passive please.

Let's march throughout the land.

There's violent crimes occurring

closer to your street.

You're scared and feeling vulnerable.

Where's the bobbies on the beat?

There could be repercussions

if you share your fears about.

You're sure that other people

will get it sorted out.

They're taking full advantage.

They know we hate to fuss.

They take great satisfaction

from the passiveness of us.

Changes will not happen

unless we make a stand.

No more massive passive please.

Let's march throughout the land.

Smoking is not healthy,

but now there's little choice.

Freedom's disappearing

so too has our voice!

You question all injustice

and though you're full of hate;

you dont want to cause bother

or things to escalate.

They're taking full advantage.

They know we hate to fuss.

They take great satisfaction

from the passiveness of us.

Changes will not happen

unless we make a stand.

No more massive passive please.

Let's march throughout the land.

THE CLEETHORPES TREATY

Politicians got their

treaties mixed up.

They agreed for

Cleethorpes to be

the capital of Europe,

and for Jedward

to be the new president.

There was no referendum.

'The Sun' was appalled

because they had no influence over it.

They shifted their allegiances

to Skegness and

'Strictly Come Dancing' instead.

OBSESSIVE OBESITY

Obsessive obesity was your profession.

You tried to eat the internet.

Tabloid Cliff Richard's dismissed your condition.

Obsessive obesity was your profession.

Nothing would sway you from your position.

You died on the Big Brother set.

Obsessive obesity was your profession.

You choked on your own silhouette.

DISTURBING

Hardbacks gathered pace
as they neared your hedgehog face.

You rubbed your chin upon the wood
(even sex was not that good.)

Splintered skin
was just your thing.

The ledge was banged
with palm of hand.

Books on Freud and Brahms
plummeted into your arms.

Where's the help for your shelf-harm
when you fought in Afghanistan?

TRAMPOLINE TRAMPLING

Invented so we'd all forget
the billions that we are in debt;
you aren't allowed to bounce,
just trample -
Johnny Vegas dancing
is a very good example.

Adolescents make us proud
as they trample, trample loud.
Winning gold's throughout the sport
mainly as we don't export
it anywhere around the world
except for Lapland.

AND THEN I CAUSED AN ACCIDENT

A lorry driver caused a crash,

not many were surviving.

A question on his lorry read –

'How safely was I driving?'

I rang the number straightaway

and told them he must be:-

'The greatest driver ever.

He swerved away from me!'

"EAT YOUR HEART OUT DAVID BLAINE"

Escaping from a tea-bag

easily,

you walked into a box

of matches

with minimum publicity.

You burst in flames,

but survived.

"Eat your heart out David Blaine,"

you cried.

Blaine did in triumph

before he slumped.

It was to be his final stunt!

You seem to love me mainly when I start to paint the shed,

decorate the living room and buy a brand new bed.

I tend to love you mainly when I'm watching Sky Sports News,

listening to Stelling and all Paul Merson's Views.

You seem to love me mainly when I'm settling the bill,

sleeping on the sofa, or thinking of my will.

I tend to love you mainly when I'm watching England beat

any other country, though it tends to be defeat.

You seem to love me mainly when I'm rarely in the house,

or relocating spiders and chasing out a mouse.

I tend to love you mainly when I'm watching Champions League,

the F.A Cup, La Liga and all the Premier League.

You seem to love me greater now you're packing up and going,

but firstly, hand the title back you've taken from this poem!

ALWAYS GETTING IT WRONG

I somersaulted from a shed

into a bowl of gruel.

You didn't seem to care.

How could you be so cruel?

It wasn't done for charity,

but as your birthday gift.

I would have bought you diamonds

if I'd known you'd be so miffed!

A LIFE CHANGING DECISION

You travelled all the way from Spain
to visit your dream 'user name'
located in the state of Maine.

He's sexy, bright and 6 ft 2.
(He says he's so in love with you.)
So what else were you meant to do?

You separated from Miguel,
and sold your children's toys as well,
so tremble as you ring the bell.

He welcomes you – it's far too late.
He's wrinkled, bald and out of date.
His picture was from '98!

i-LIFE...

You're qualified but have to wait
until you get your lucky break.
You stay in your pyjamas everyday.

And other jobs you've ever read
will hardly ever pay the rent.
You smell the mould aroma every day.

    You can't do work unless it fits your dream.
    It's not your fault that life's a trampoline.

You fill your half days
with your i-ways.
You chat to i-mates
and make some i-dates.
You tweet your i-dea
and drink your i-beer.
You have an i-wife
and live the i-life.
You live the i-life.

You don't attempt to venture out.
Cloudy skies just make you doubt
yourself and future prospects even more.
Your father doesn't understand
and says get out and be a man.
Where most see illness he just sees a flaw.

　　You can't do work unless it fits your dream.
　　Your state is down-bounce on a trampoline.

You fill your half days
with your i-ways.
You chat to i-mates
and make some i-dates.
You tweet your i-dea
and drink your i-beer.
You have an i-wife
and live the i-life.

You live the i-life.
But not the high life.

DIPLOMATIC WITH THE TRUTH

We meet

in the street,

and though I can tell –

I ask if you're well.

"Fine thanks," you reply

(being polite)

despite

walking by

with a spluttering cough,

your arm in a sling

and a patch on one eye!

MOTHER'S PRIDE

Beer belly clouds

lop over the horizon

wearing the landscape like jeans.

Fog thickening

like arteries

devours hope,

consuming memories.

The diabetic sky

collapses

in relief,

and wets itself.

FRUSTRATION

You seduced the moon,
undressing it with your soul.

You tortured it with
anticipation.

You could never unite.

Long distance
relationships
were not your thing.

BLACK ICE PEAS

Slipping,
tripping,
ripping,
back of pack
of frozen peas.

Will.I.Am
was not best pleased.

He slammed
a can
of spam
and shouted
'Damn!'

Then threw
his shoe
and banger
in anger
as he looked above
pleading 'Where Is The Love?'

No 47 Arsenal.... will play.....Yellow Ticket
Number 237 (Mrs Angela HobNob)

"A DELL – NOT ADELE!"

'I love to hear her songs

but you got my order wrong.

I did not want 'Adele'

but 'A Dell',

'A Dell' PC I tell you!

I needed CPU,

Windows and some RAM,

not 'Someone Like You'

from an international star

who came to Jam

and be PC

just because she thought that's what I wanted.'

[THIS POEM WAS ABANDONED AT HALF-TIME
DUE TO A BISCUIT SHORTAGE]

ON GOOD ADVICE

I broke my leg but couldn't claim

(I failed to sign the form again!)

I was however not to blame.

[FOR LEGAL REASONS I CANNOT CONTINUE]

MISLED

You said she was a 'porn' star,
but the 'porning' she excelled in
was 'pawnbrokering'.

She rarely took her clothes off
but took away my watch each night,
threatening to keep it
if I tried to kiss her.

QUIZ OFF

You win each quiz. It's so irritating.

We want to win – give us a chance.

Soon only you will be participating.

You win each quiz. It's so irritating.

We try a new quiz. You're there. It's frustrating.

You practice your victory dance.

You win each quiz. It's so irritating.

We want to win – give us a chance.

MINCE PI

The smell was slightly different.

My taste buds felt so glum.

I can't believe I'd eaten

3 point 141.

USE THIS SPACE AS AN EMERGENCY ICE RINK

THE CLOUD SHOP

IS PROUD TO SPONSOR WHATEVER THE NAME OF THIS BOOK IS.

PRECIPITATION SALE NOW ON.

CIRRUS CLOUDS ARE ALL HALF PRICE.

CUMULUS CLOUDS ON A STICK ARE NOW RANDOM PRICES.

BE QUICK BEFORE WE GET CLOSED DOWN.

THE CLOUD SHOP

(The Shop without a slogan.)

HAIKU HELL

THE ASTRONAUT

Fearless astronaut

speeding through black wilderness

on the underground.

THE ATHLETE

Olympic athlete

smashes his personal best

when chasing the bus.

THE VENTRILOQUIST

The Ventriloquist

throws his voice around again.

His dummy drops it.

THE SIT-DOWN STAND-UP

The drunk, moronic comic
sat down to do his set;
heckled all the audience
and gestured as he left.

Most remained and cheered,
whilst those who stood and jeered
failed to see the irony!

THE TITLE IS THE FIRST LINE

You took your trousers off in the middle of Coronation Street.

You thought that Gail needed a treat.

She wasn't even in the episode.

The Beckham's never invited you around again!

EXCLUSIVE

UNFAIR DISMISSAL

'I was the weakest link,' she yelled.

'You're sacked. Get out. Goodbye!'

(She wanted apple strudel,

not a steak and kidney pie.)

REINSTATED

The steak and kidney pie was good.

She text me with the news.

'Have ur job back + a rise,

then nething u choose.'

SACKED AGAIN

The message came to me too late.

In anger I'd gone mad.

I smashed up half the office

and burnt the files I had.

BAD TIMING

The documentary camera team

told me 'Don't despair.

Now you will be famous'-

(I forgot that they were there!)

SABOTAGE

A toffee apple won the race

followed by a lime.

(I think a rival poet

is ruining my rhyme.)

RECORD RATINGS

I had a peak-time series.

A song called 'Office Nutter'.

The tabloids were all jealous

and left me in the gutter.

THE MEANING OF LIFE

The moral of this poem –

Third was bread and jam.

The meaning of our lives is this –

Fourth was Desperate Dan.

A SWIFT RECOVERY

Leaving after

    40 years.

        The manager

            broke down in tears.

                His RAC colleagues

                    picked him up.

ROCK SINGING FISH FINGERS – A MEMORIAL

One Sunday night I heard a knock,

receiving such a mighty shock –

fish fingers playing country rock.

Out of tune, it was quite poor,

I tried to clear them from my door –

but somehow they performed one more.

I tried to give them some advice.

They didn't listen. I got spice.

And ate them up – which wasn't nice.

Fish finger eating is allowed

but sometimes it don't make me proud

the way I gobbled up that crowd.

Their cousins say that I will pay –

I'm threatened nearly every day

by fish cake mobs who want their way.

But now I don't eat food with fins,

preferring fruit and veg in tins –

thank goodness God forgave my sins –

Hallelujah!

THE POEM PEDLAR

Skipping on stilts

and tripping on sonnets.

You pushed your rhymes upon us.

A line of Larkin,

cuts of Blake,

made my state

hallucinate.

Cope consumed

and Hughes inhaled.

Stoned on Shelley,

Heaney hailed.

High on Hegley,

chilled on Clare.

Coleridge made me

breathe new air.

You threw some Dylan in the mix,

but I refused. I'd had my fix.

I soon came down, came down, so down

and thought that David Cameron

was reading Keats and making cuts

to Kipling's "If", and

BORING GEEZER

You talk about your Sunday Roast,
and how you eat your beans on toast.
You moan about your motherboard,
and how your central heating's flawed.

You talk about your favourite fish,
and ins and outs of Weetabix.
You moan about some C++.
It doesn't mean a lot to us.

Oh you're a boring geezer,
boring geezer,
boring geezer.

Oh you're a boring geezer,
boring geezer,
boring geezer.

Your traffic stories are so long
that we could play each Beatles song,
and still it wouldn't be complete.
I have to hear them all damn week!

Oh you're a boring geezer,
boring geezer,
boring geezer.

Oh you're a boring geezer,
boring geezer,
boring geezer.

And then one day you turn to me,
and say it's such a travesty,
the way I hardly say a word.
I was amazed by what I heard:-

"Oh you're a boring geezer,
boring geezer,
boring geezer.

Oh you're a boring geezer,
boring geezer,
boring geezer."

SNOOD FOR THOUGHT

There's another epidemic
spreading through the land.
More and more are wearing snoods.
I just don't understand.

I've seen them on celebrities,
the poor and on the rich.
I've seen them worn in Tesco's,
and on a football pitch.

I haven't seen them yet in darts,
or worn by any priests.
I hope a Space Invader
would ban them from the streets.

They say it is unstoppable.

I've heeded some advice,

and did what Google told me to

and had my snood jab twice!

I'M NOT THE POET LAUREATE

From: **Eric Dazzle** (poetical@hotmail.co.uk)
Sent: 18 October 2010 12:16:33
To: Taylorsmart1@hotmail.co.uk
Subject: The Importance of Being Eric Idle

Hi mate,

My name's Eric, but I'm not Eric Idle as the subject
suggests. (I just did that to be funny :-))

I loved your performance in Camden last night. I sat five
rows from the front and wore a shirt (you probably noticed
me.)

My personal favourites were 'Saggy Days' and 'Laughing
Mouse'. I wasn't too keen on 'Ranky Spanky' though, as I
thought it was too crude.

I also thought that the rhyming scheme was too clunky and
some of the lines were too contrived. Take these for
example:-

'I hate you when you're Ranky Spanky,
Why can't you be my Cranky Lanky'.

It just didn't work for me. I hope you don't mind me giving you this bit of constructive criticism (I get it all the time!)

I look forward to seeing you perform in the future (hopefully taking on board some of my criticisms!)

Kind regards,
Eric Dazzle.

P.S It was Dave who passed on your email address to me . He said it would be alright.

From: Taylor Smart (taylorsmart1@hotmail.co.uk)
Sent: 18 October 2010 14:57:57
To: poetical@hotmail.co.uk

Who the hell are you?
You're not my 'mate' as you state. I have never met you.
How dare you critisise my work when you say you are also
a poet (not a very good one by the sounds of it!!!!)

'Ranky Spanky' is satirical and if you understood it
properly you would have realised that the contrived rhyme
was deliberate.
I was satirising rubbish poetry like you probably churn out,
you dullard!

Please do not email me again. I have told Dave not to give
my email address out to dickheads like you in future.

From an annoyed artiste.

P.S - I don't think you could be funny if you tried.

From: **Eric Dazzle (poetical@hotmail.co.uk)**
Sent: **18 October 2010 17:41:19**
To: **taylorsmart1@hotmail.co.uk**

Hi Taylor,

I'm really sorry that I offended you. I have had a tough time recently. I am just getting over the death of my budgie, Seth. My brother Basil told me to stop being so wimpish and just get over it. I couldn't stop weeping for three days. He isn't too sympathetic at times and doesn't understand us sensitive souls. Mark Williams, my favourite snooker player, then got knocked out in the semi-finals of a major tournament. It was another set-back I had to endure. I thought everything was turning around when I heard the Poetry Society was planning to host a 'Poetry Idol' event. This soon turned to disappointment though as they told me the rumour was false.

Sorry to burden you with these woes Taylor. You don't mind me calling you Taylor do you? (It is your name after all.)

I googled you to see if I could find any of your poems on the internet so I could write a favourable review, even if it wasn't entirely true.

I couldn't see you on there. Perhaps you are allergic to the internet like I am. Aitchoo! (A feather caused that rather than the internet!)

Hope we are friends now.

Would you like me to send you one of my poems?

Eric

From: Taylor Smart (taylorsmart1@hotmail.co.uk)
Sent: 26 October 2010 09:24:03
To: poetical@hotmail.co.uk

Hi Eric,

Really sorry to hear about your budgie. I have five of my own but lost one earlier in the year, so know what you are going through. What breed was it? Do you have any others?
Your brother sounds really insensitive.

Although I was upset by your first email, I am willing to forgive you as a result of what you've told me.

I must admit I'm not really into snooker, but have heard of Mark Williams. Is he the 'Rocket' by any chance?

I would have been very surprised if the Poetry Society had been thinking of organising something as downmarket as a 'Poetry Idol' event.

So what kind of poetry do you write? I'm interested in reading some now.

There may be a chance of us becoming friends, but only if you're not too quick to critisise my work.

Taylor

From: Eric Dazzle (poetical@hotmail.co.uk)
Sent: 26 October 2010 09:51:44
To: taylorsmart1@hotmail.co.uk

Hi Taylor.

Thanks for your reply. It meant a lot to me.
If you don't mind I will probably print out your email 30
times and stick each one on my wall.
It may help me sleep.

Yes, I've got another budgie. It's called Noel, after Noel
Edmonds. This is mainly because its plumage reminds me
of one of the hideous sweaters Noel used to wear on Telly
Addicts.

Are you into any other sports then? I like most apart from
'The Discus', 'Rock Climbing Aerobics', and of course –
'Bobbling'.

Ronnie O'Sullivan is nicknamed the 'Rocket'. I think
Williams is nicknamed the 'Wilderbeest', 'Wingspan',
'Wagon Wheel' or something else beginning with 'W'.

Here is one of my poems:-

TOAST

You make me toast.
I eat it.
You make me tea.
I drink it.
You make me toast.
I eat it.
You make me toast.
I eat it.
You make me toast.
I eat it.

You make me toast.
I don't eat it this time as I'm rather full up and fed up of toast now.

Cheers,
Eric.

P.S – I hope you don't mind me being critical one more time, but you spell criticise wrong. It is 'criticise' and not 'critisise'.

From:
Taylor Smart (taylorsmart1@hotmail.co.uk)
Sent: 26 October 2010 12:12:37
To: poetical@hotmail.co.uk

I don't know what to make of you at times Eric.

I was a bit freaked when you said you would stick 30 copies
of my email on your wall.
I then laughed out loud when you said you had
named your budgie Noel, after Noel Edmonds.

I like swimming and hockey. What exactly is bobbling?!!

Your poem is unusual too.

Against my better judgment, I would like to know about
you. Are you married? If not, are you in the 25-35 age
bracket? Would you like to meet up for a drink?
(I will have to speak to you on the phone first though) I
will give you my number if you give me yours.

Taylor
x

P.S – No hard feelings about 'criticise'. Thanks for letting
me know.

From:
Eric Dazzle (poetical@hotmail.co.uk)
Sent: 28 October 2010 10:12:43
To: taylorsmart1@hotmail.co.uk

Dating! Are you sure? I'm no Gruffalo, but I'm no Wayne Rooney either.

I am in the age bracket you mention, but have never been asked out for a date before.

I usually do the asking and never hear back.

I will be delighted to meet up with you for a drink.

I have big bushy eyebrows and a fake eye. If that does not put you off then I will give you my number.

I may have to buy some aftershave from Poundland so I can smell my best.

Yours excitedly,

Eric

END OF CORRESPONDENCE

THE CARPET WAREHOUSE

The Dazzle (poetic..

Sent: 22 October 2

To:

From: Eric Dazzle (poetical@hotmail.co.uk)
Sent: 19 September 2010 14:34:27
To: sales@thecarpetwarehouse.co.uk

Dear Sir/Dame,

May I firstly congratulate you on your website. It is pretty
good.

Secondly, I have just seen a stunning carpet I would like to
order.

I am rather struggling for cash at the moment, though, due
to an unfortunate accident involving a banana skin while
re-enacting a comedy scene from a 1970s sit-com.

I know this sounds daft, but would you consider taking
other forms of payment such as gold, jewellery, or poems?

Yesterday I was able to purchase a dustpan and brush in
exchange for three limericks I had written. I do know more
and more companies are starting to accept alternative
payments for goods due to the harsh economic climate.

I feel really embarassed for asking (and will try and cadge some money off an old relative if necessary) but I do really like the carpet.

Kind regards,
Eric Dazzle

END OF CORRESPONDENCE

TREVOR BAYLISS BRANDS

From: Eric Dazzle (poetical@hotmail.co.uk)
Sent: 09 October 2010 12:38:15
To: business@trevorbaylisbrands.com

Hi,

I wonder if you can provide me with some advice please.

I have just come up with an idea that combines poetry with traditional musical theatre to form the 'Poeical'.

Instead of songs, the 'Poeical' would have poems instead. To mix it up some characters would use limericks, some sonnets, some rondeau's and some haikus. Some characters would also use my new poetic form called the 'Rhyponda'. This poetic form has 17 lines consisting of an 'a,b,c,d,e,d,d,b,a,a,g,f,f,d,c,b,e' rhyming scheme.

What do I do next to ensure my idea does not get stolen by a blaggard?

Kind regards,
Eric Dazzle

From: business
(business@trevorbaylisbrands.com)
Sent: 11 October 2010 09:13:15
To: Eric Dazzle (poetical@hotmail.co.uk)

Dear Mr Dazzle,

Thank you for your enquiry. Any work of art or authorship is automatically protected by copyright. Any documents that you produce that describe your ideas will automatically have this protection.

You could also contemplate creating a trade mark for 'Poeical' although that would need a careful consideration of the Trade Mark rules. You can find these on http://www.ipo.gov.uk

We hope that this answer is helpful.

Trevor Baylis Brands plc

From: Eric Dazzle (poetical@hotmail.co.uk)
Sent: 13 October 2010 19:56:22
To: business@trevorbaylisbrands.com

Brilliant.

Thank you very much dude.

Do you provide any feedback on ideas?

Give me your honest opinion. Do you think the last 342 days has been wasted on this concept?

I feel I'm nearly there, but at the same time continue to get frustrated as there always seems to be another hurdle to overcome

Eric 'The' Dazzle

From: business (business@trevorbaylisbrands.com)
Sent: 14 October 2010 11:56:59
To: Eric Dazzle (poetical@hotmail.co.uk)

Dear Mr Dazzle,

Time spent in creative activity is never wasted and there should be more of it.
Frequently getting things to fruition is about stamina not creativity, so if you believe in your idea you should hang on in there.

We hope that this helps.
Trevor Baylis Brands plc

From: Eric Dazzle (poetical@hotmail.co.uk)
Sent: 17 October 2010 09:32:30
To: business@trevorbaylisbrands.com

Dear Trevor Baylis Brands plc,

Thank you so much for your kind response.
It almost made me cry into my egg and chips (I was just
about to have lunch when I read your lovely email.)

I am much more confident now that the last 346 days have
not been a waste after all.

Kind regards,
Eric

END OF CORRESPONDENCE

An Idea To Reduce The Number of

Red Cards in Football

To info@amateur-fa.com

From: Eric Dazzle (poetical@hotmail.co.uk)

Sent: 27 April 2011 00:22:12

To: info@amateur-fa.com

Dear Madam/Sir,

I have a revolutionary idea to reduce the number of red cards in football, and thus improve discipline within the sport.

Instead of being sent off for one or two misdemeanours, a player should spend 10 minutes reciting poetry over the public address system.

This would humiliate the player, and thus deter them from committing offences in the future.

Alternatively, the player could be forced to sit with opposition fans and compose a chant criticising one of their own team-mates.

Many of my friends think it is a ridiculous idea, but I think some of the best ideas in the past have been ridiculed at some point - i.e. Hopscotch.

If you decide to implement this suggestion then I would not require a cash payment, just a bottle of Harvey's Bristol Cream Sherry.

Kind Regards,
Eric

END OF CORRESPONDENCE